DANGER BELOW!

FLOATING MISERY!

PORTUGUESE MAN-OF-WAR ATTACK

BY JAMES BUCKLEY JR.

ILLUSTRATED BY CASSIE ANDERSON

BEARPORT
PUBLISHING

Minneapolis, Minnesota

Credits

20T © Wild and Free Naturephoto/Shutterstock; 20B © Anokato/Shutterstock; 21 © Sciencepics/Shutterstock; 22T © Richard Whitcombe/Shutterstock; 22B © John A. Anderson/Shutterstock.

Produced by Shoreline Publishing Group LLC
Santa Barbara, California
Designer: Patty Kelley
Editorial Director: James Buckley Jr.

DISCLAIMER: This graphic story is a dramatization based on true events. It is intended to give the reader a sense of the narrative rather than a presentation of actual details as they occurred.

Library of Congress Cataloging-in-Publication Data

Names: Buckley, James, Jr., 1963– author. | Anderson, Cassie, illustrator.
Title: Floating misery! : Portuguese man-of-war attack / by James Buckley
    Jr. ; illustrated by Cassie Anderson.
Description: Bear claw edition. | Minneapolis, Minnesota : Bearport
    Publishing, [2021] | Series: Danger below! | Includes bibliographical
    references and index.
Identifiers: LCCN 2020008651 (print) | LCCN 2020008652 (ebook) | ISBN
    9781647470524 (library binding) | ISBN 9781647470593 (paperback) | ISBN
    9781647470661 (ebook)
Subjects: LCSH: Portuguese man-of-war—Juvenile literature. | Portuguese
    man-of-war—Comic books, strips, etc. | Graphic novels.
Classification: LCC QL377.H9 B83 2021 (print) | LCC QL377.H9 (ebook) |
    DDC 593.5/5—dc23
LC record available at https://lccn.loc.gov/2020008651
LC ebook record available at https://lccn.loc.gov/2020008652

For more information, write to Bearport Publishing, 5357 Penn Avenue South, Minneapolis, MN 55419. Printed in the United States of America.

CONTENTS

CHAPTER 1

TROUBLE IN THE WIND

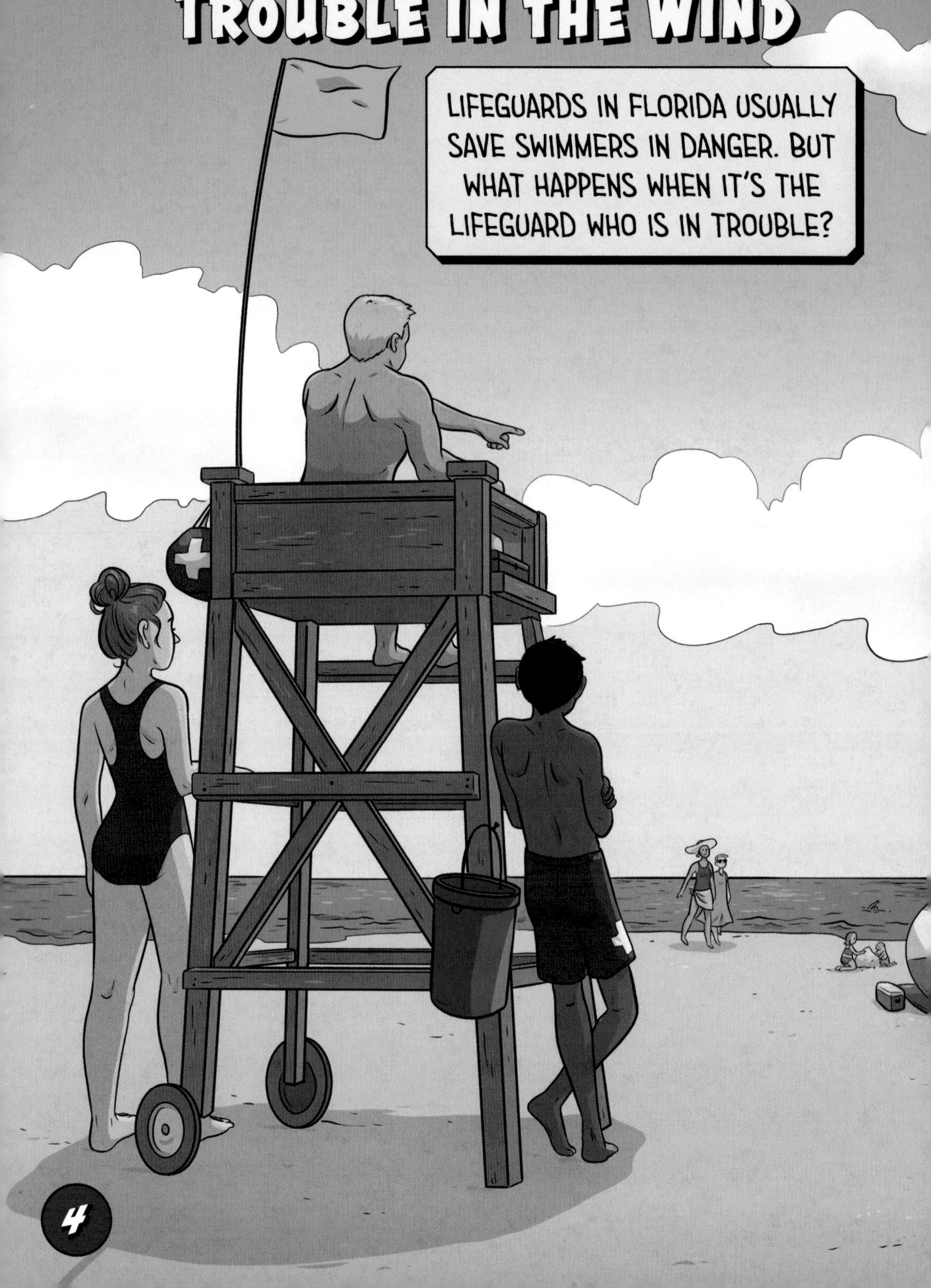
LIFEGUARDS IN FLORIDA USUALLY SAVE SWIMMERS IN DANGER. BUT WHAT HAPPENS WHEN IT'S THE LIFEGUARD WHO IS IN TROUBLE?

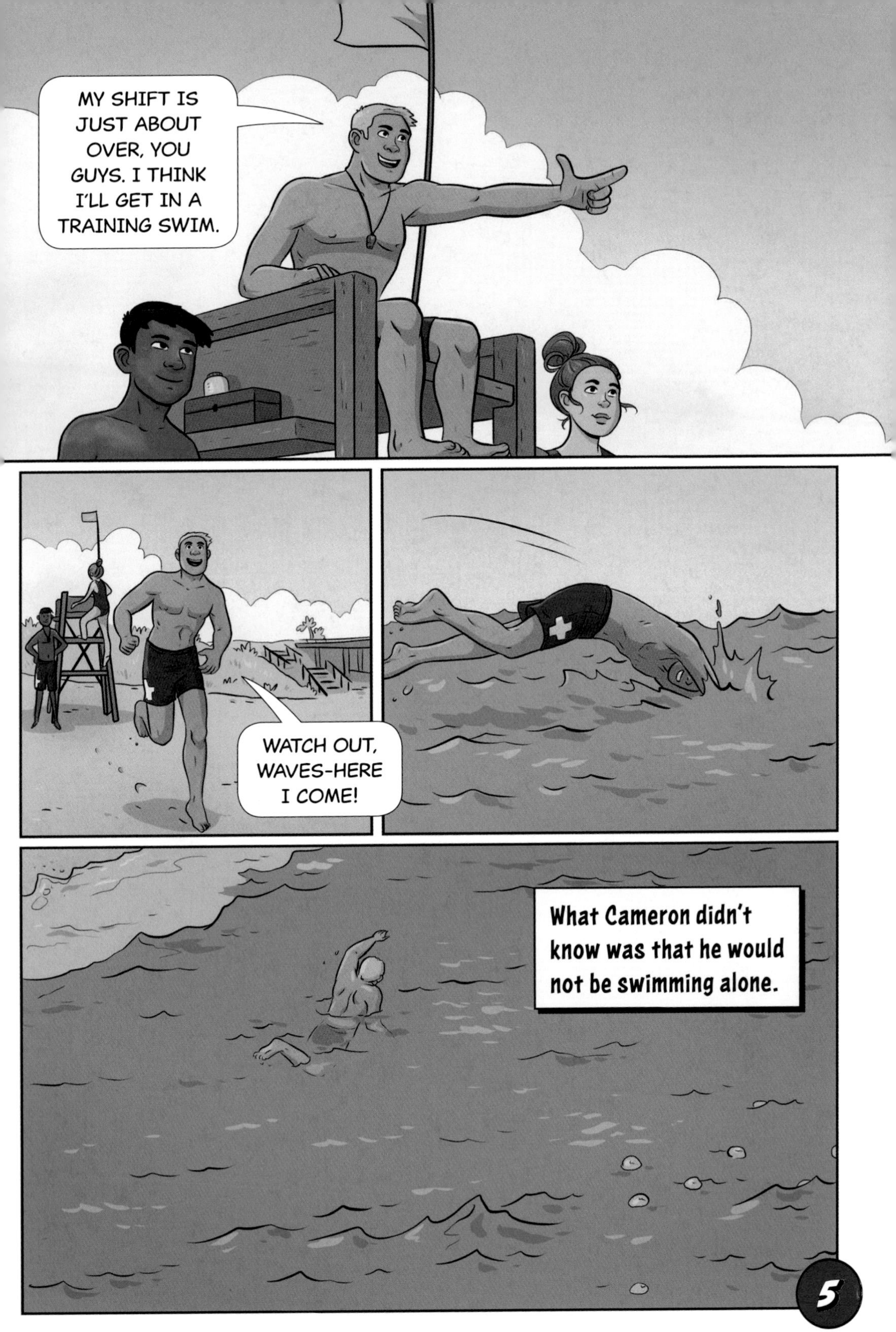
MY SHIFT IS JUST ABOUT OVER, YOU GUYS. I THINK I'LL GET IN A TRAINING SWIM.
WATCH OUT, WAVES-HERE I COME!
What Cameron didn't know was that he would not be swimming alone.

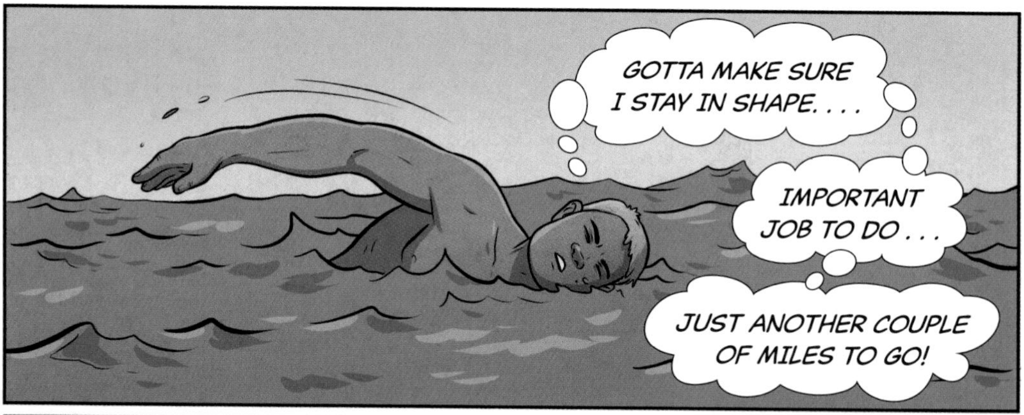
GOTTA MAKE SURE I STAY IN SHAPE. . . .
IMPORTANT JOB TO DO . . .
JUST ANOTHER COUPLE OF MILES TO GO!

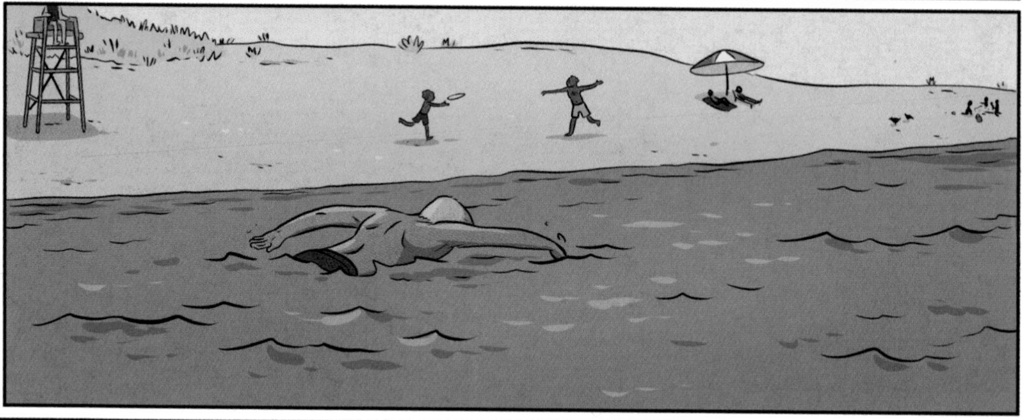

Lifeguards raise flags to tell beachgoers about the water conditions.

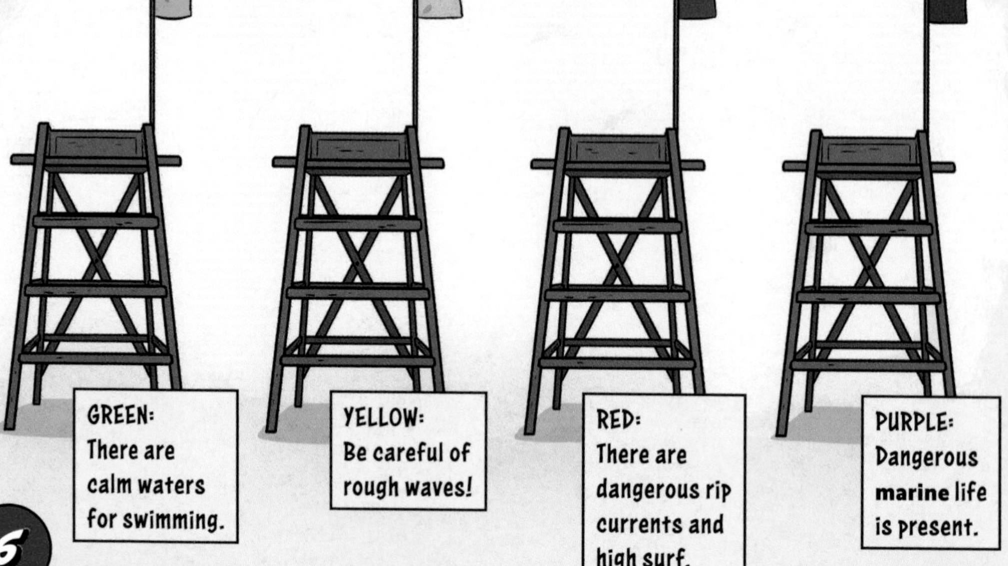
GREEN:
There are calm waters for swimming.
YELLOW:
Be careful of rough waves!
RED:
There are dangerous rip currents and high surf.
PURPLE:
Dangerous **marine** life is present.

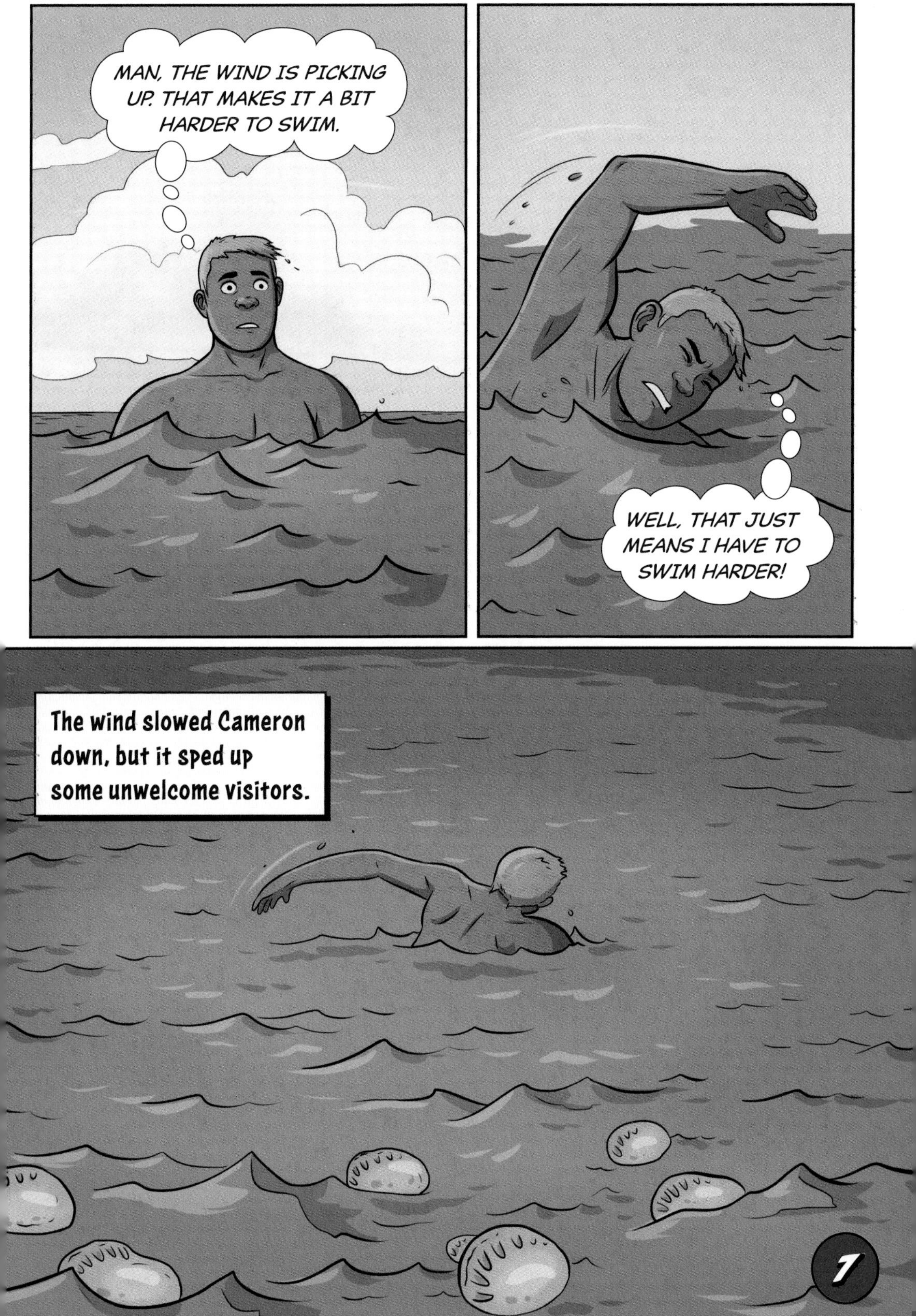
MAN, THE WIND IS PICKING UP. THAT MAKES IT A BIT HARDER TO SWIM.
WELL, THAT JUST MEANS I HAVE TO SWIM HARDER!
The wind slowed Cameron down, but it sped up some unwelcome visitors.

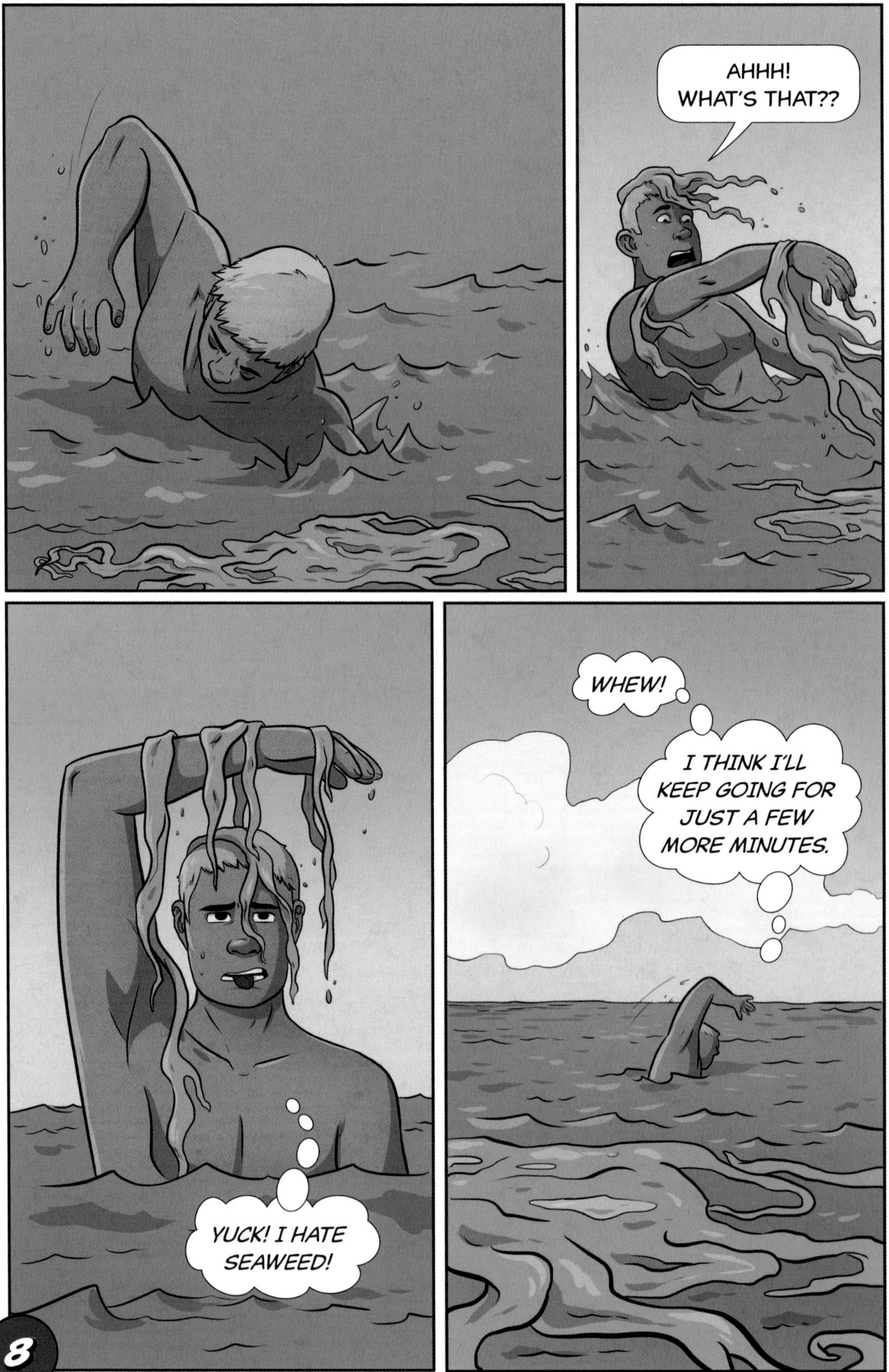
AHHH!
WHAT'S THAT??
YUCK! I HATE SEAWEED!
WHEW!
I THINK I'LL KEEP GOING FOR JUST A FEW MORE MINUTES.

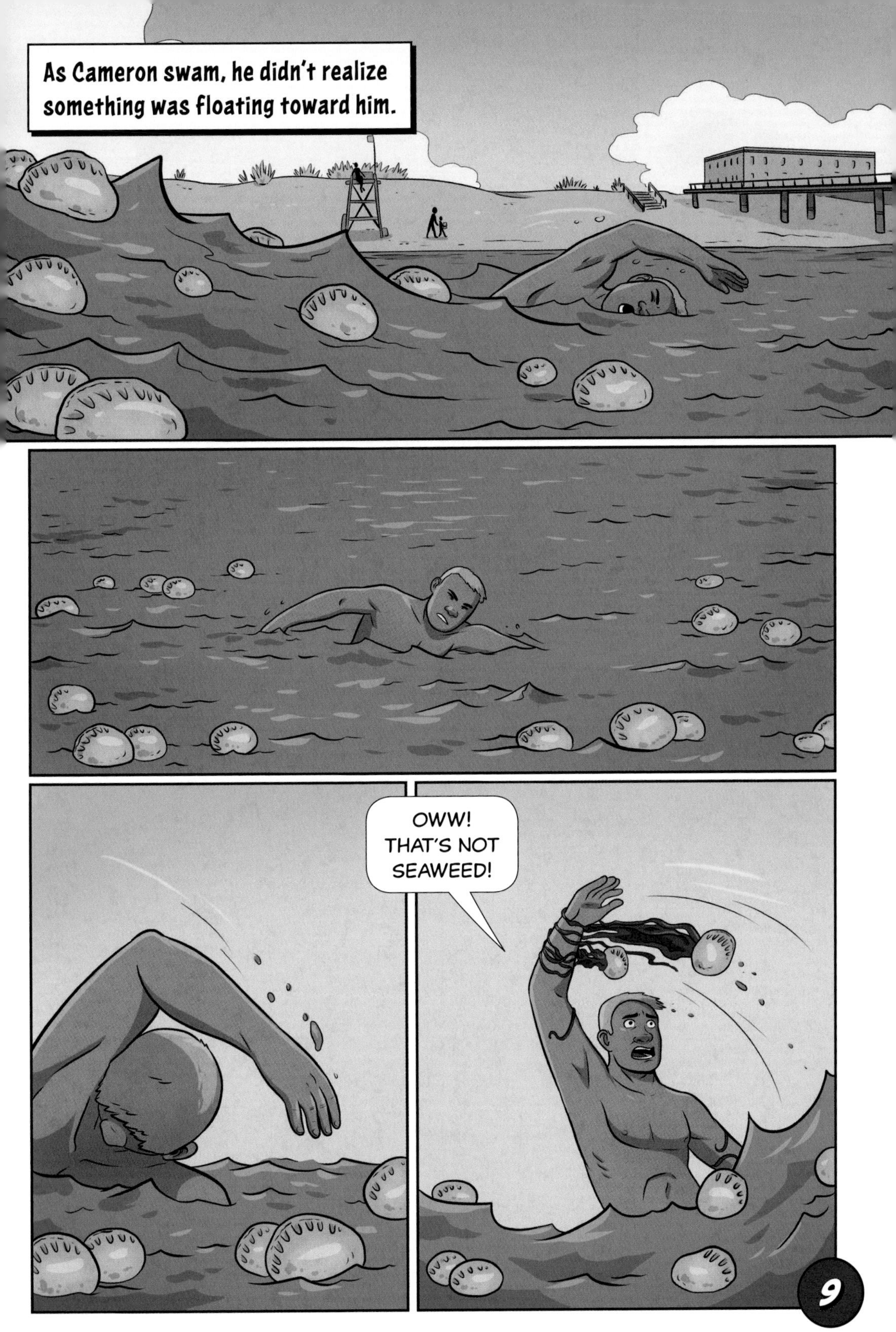
As Cameron swam, he didn't realize something was floating toward him.
OWW! THAT'S NOT SEAWEED!

CHAPTER 2

TANGLED IN TENTACLES

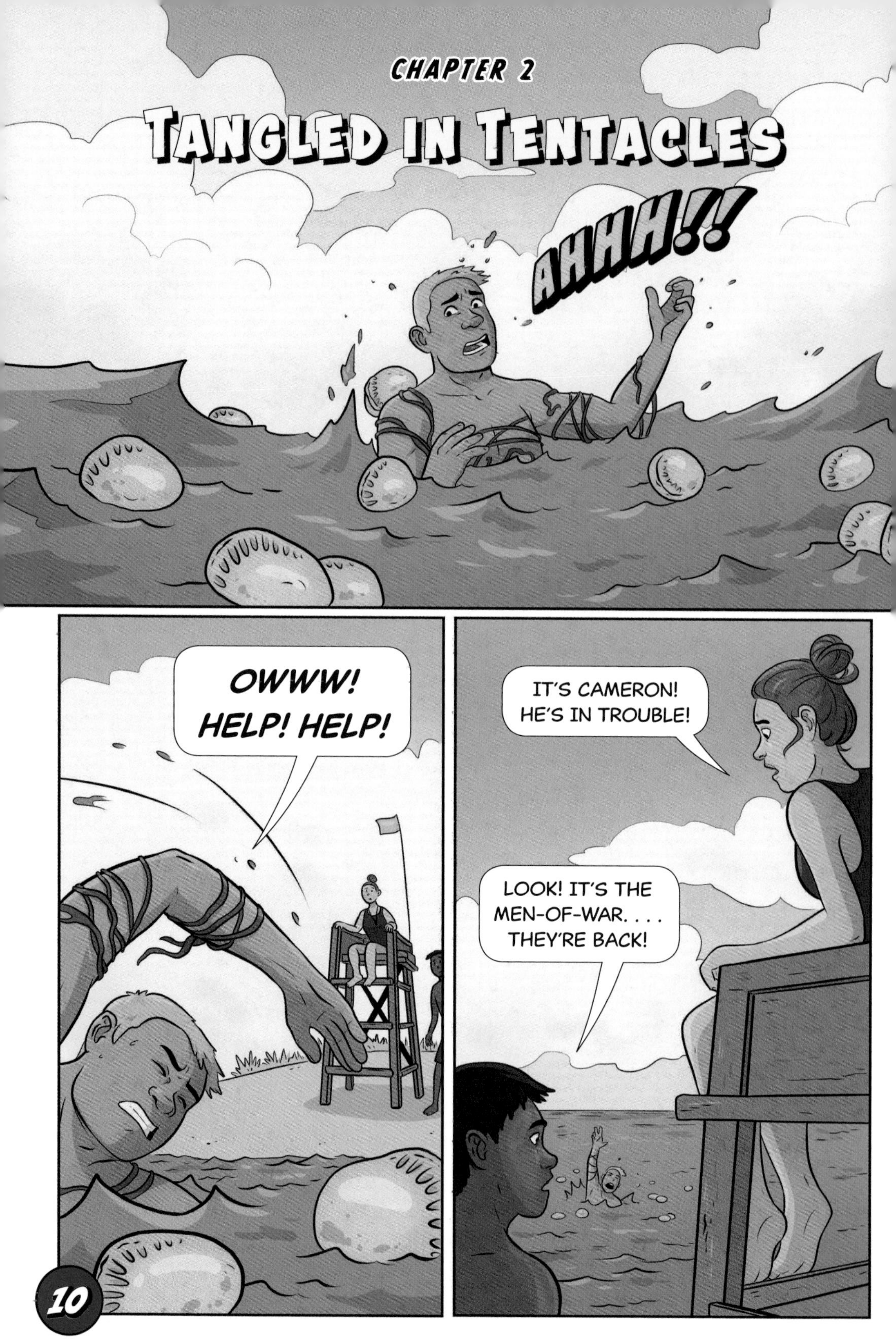
AHHH!!
OWWW! HELP! HELP!
IT'S CAMERON! HE'S IN TROUBLE!
LOOK! IT'S THE MEN-OF-WAR. . . . THEY'RE BACK!

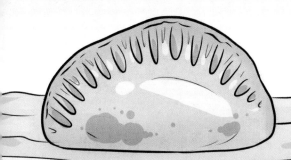

Cameron had become entangled in a dangerous sea creature called a Portuguese man-of-war. The **tentacles** that wrapped around him were covered with stingers. The man-of-war uses the stingers to **paralyze** its **prey**. Tangling a human like Cameron in its tentacles was just an accident!

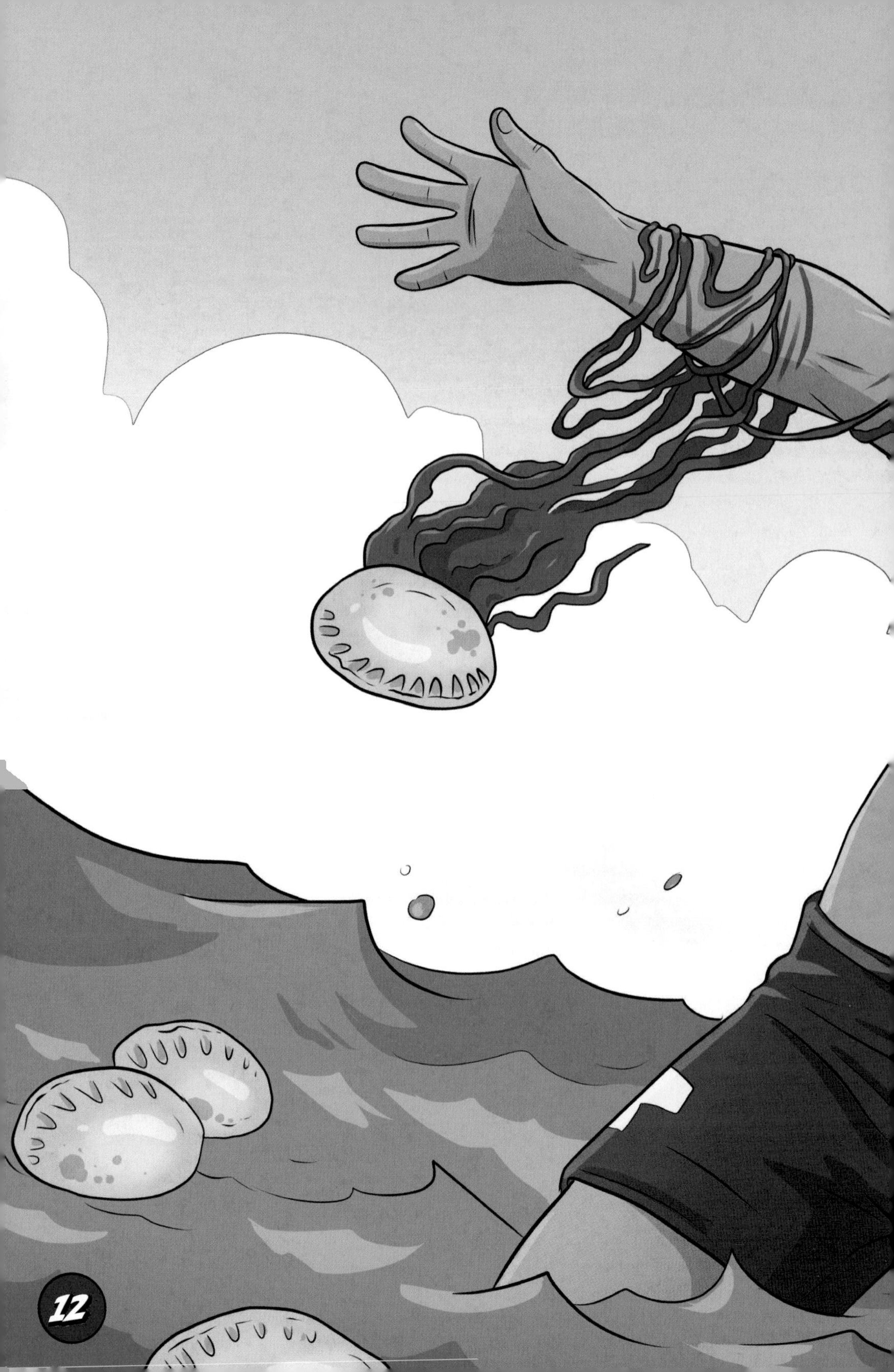

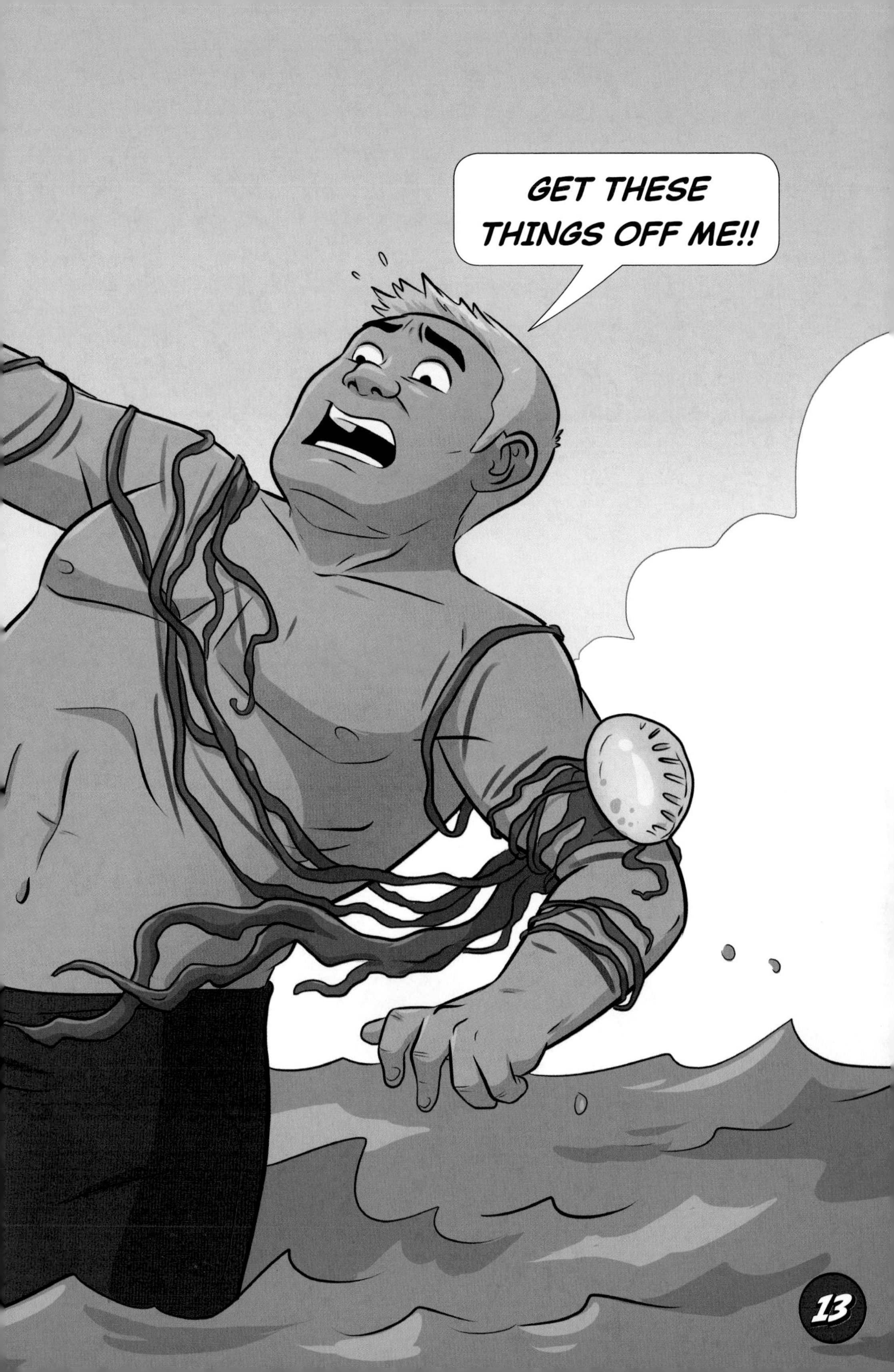
GET THESE THINGS OFF ME!!

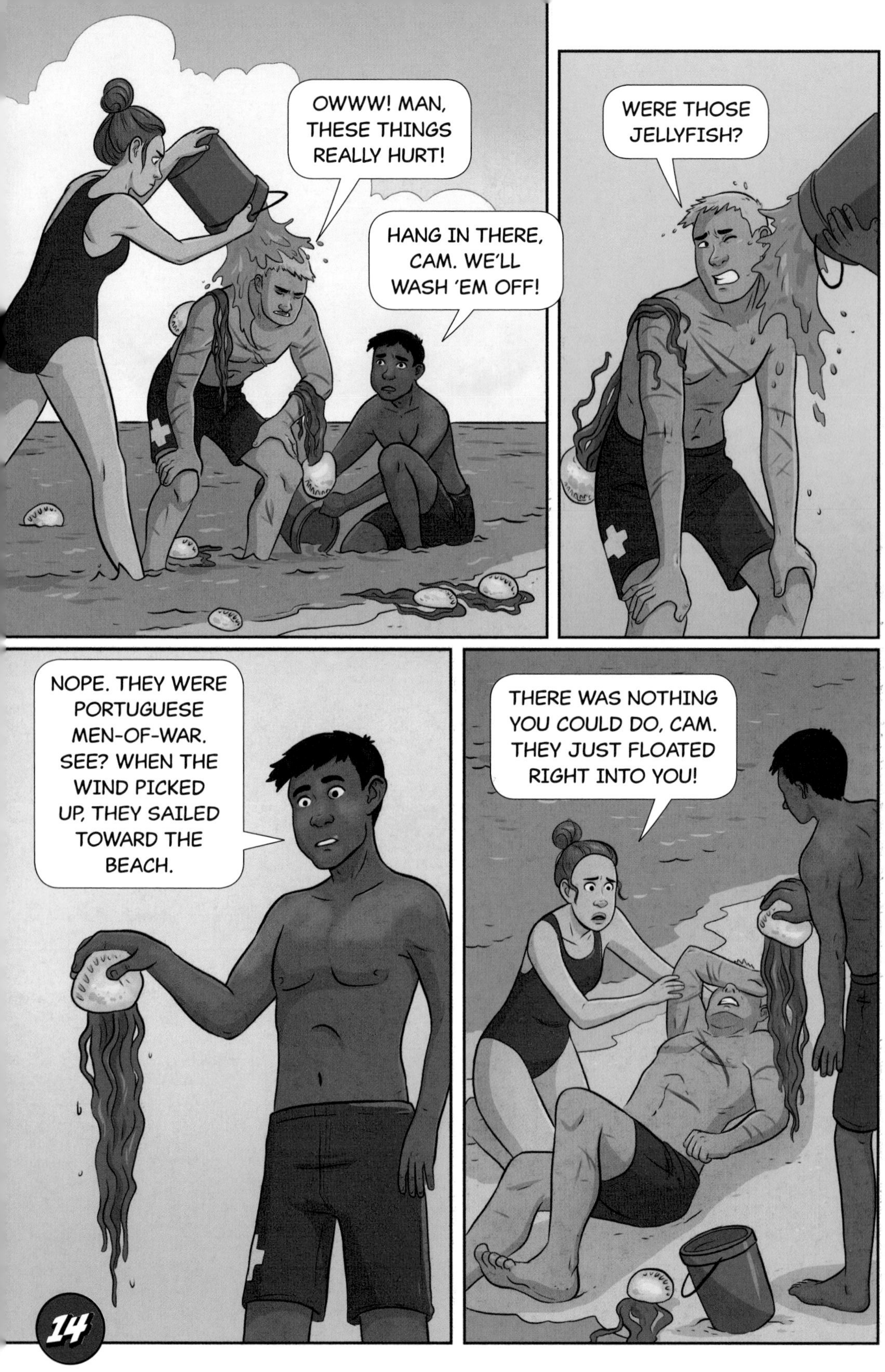
OWWW! MAN, THESE THINGS REALLY HURT!
HANG IN THERE, CAM. WE'LL WASH 'EM OFF!
WERE THOSE JELLYFISH?
NOPE. THEY WERE PORTUGUESE MEN-OF-WAR. SEE? WHEN THE WIND PICKED UP, THEY SAILED TOWARD THE BEACH.
THERE WAS NOTHING YOU COULD DO, CAM. THEY JUST FLOATED RIGHT INTO YOU!

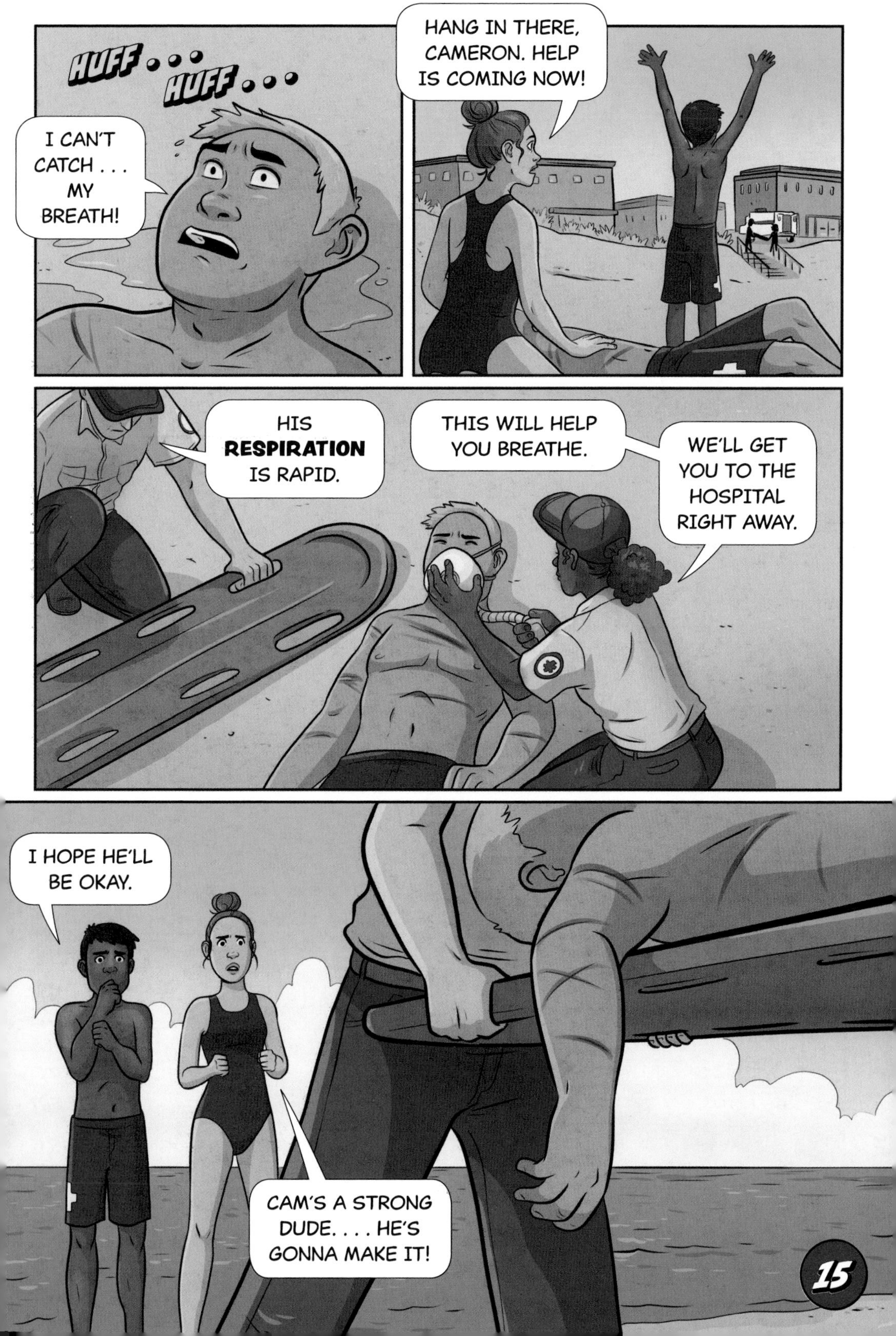
HUFF . . .
HUFF . . .
I CAN'T CATCH . . . MY BREATH!
HANG IN THERE, CAMERON. HELP IS COMING NOW!
HIS **RESPIRATION** IS RAPID.
THIS WILL HELP YOU BREATHE.
WE'LL GET YOU TO THE HOSPITAL RIGHT AWAY.
I HOPE HE'LL BE OKAY.
CAM'S A STRONG DUDE. . . . HE'S GONNA MAKE IT!

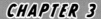

CHAPTER 3

SAFE AT LAST?

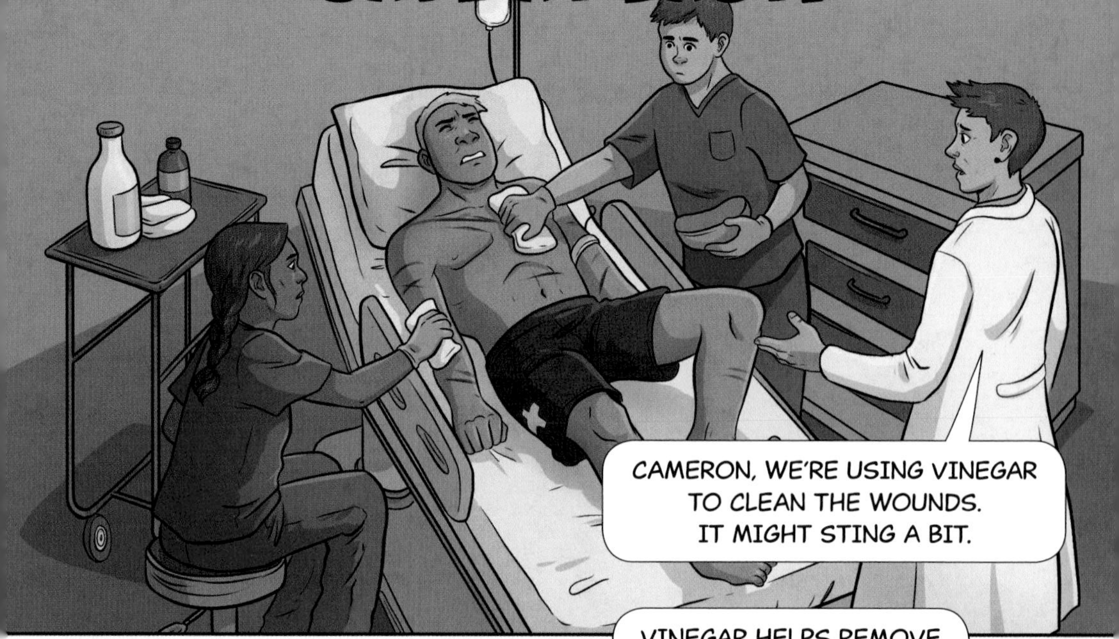
CAMERON, WE'RE USING VINEGAR TO CLEAN THE WOUNDS. IT MIGHT STING A BIT.

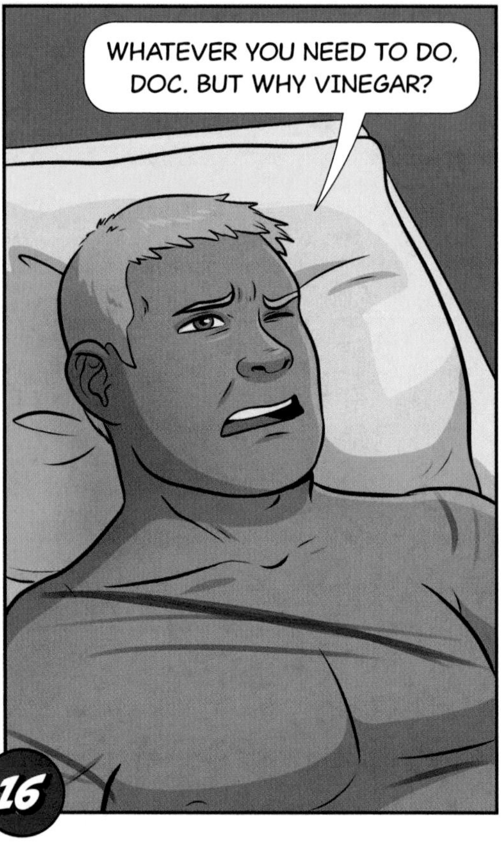
WHATEVER YOU NEED TO DO, DOC. BUT WHY VINEGAR?

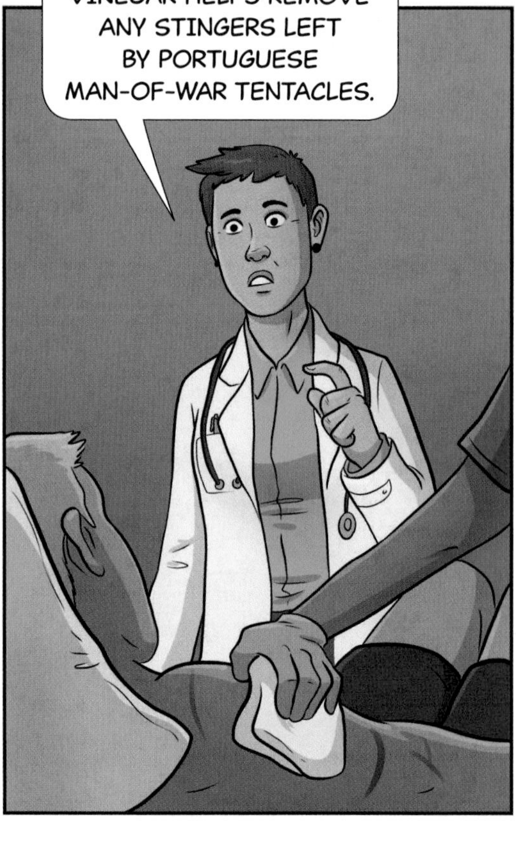
VINEGAR HELPS REMOVE ANY STINGERS LEFT BY PORTUGUESE MAN-OF-WAR TENTACLES.

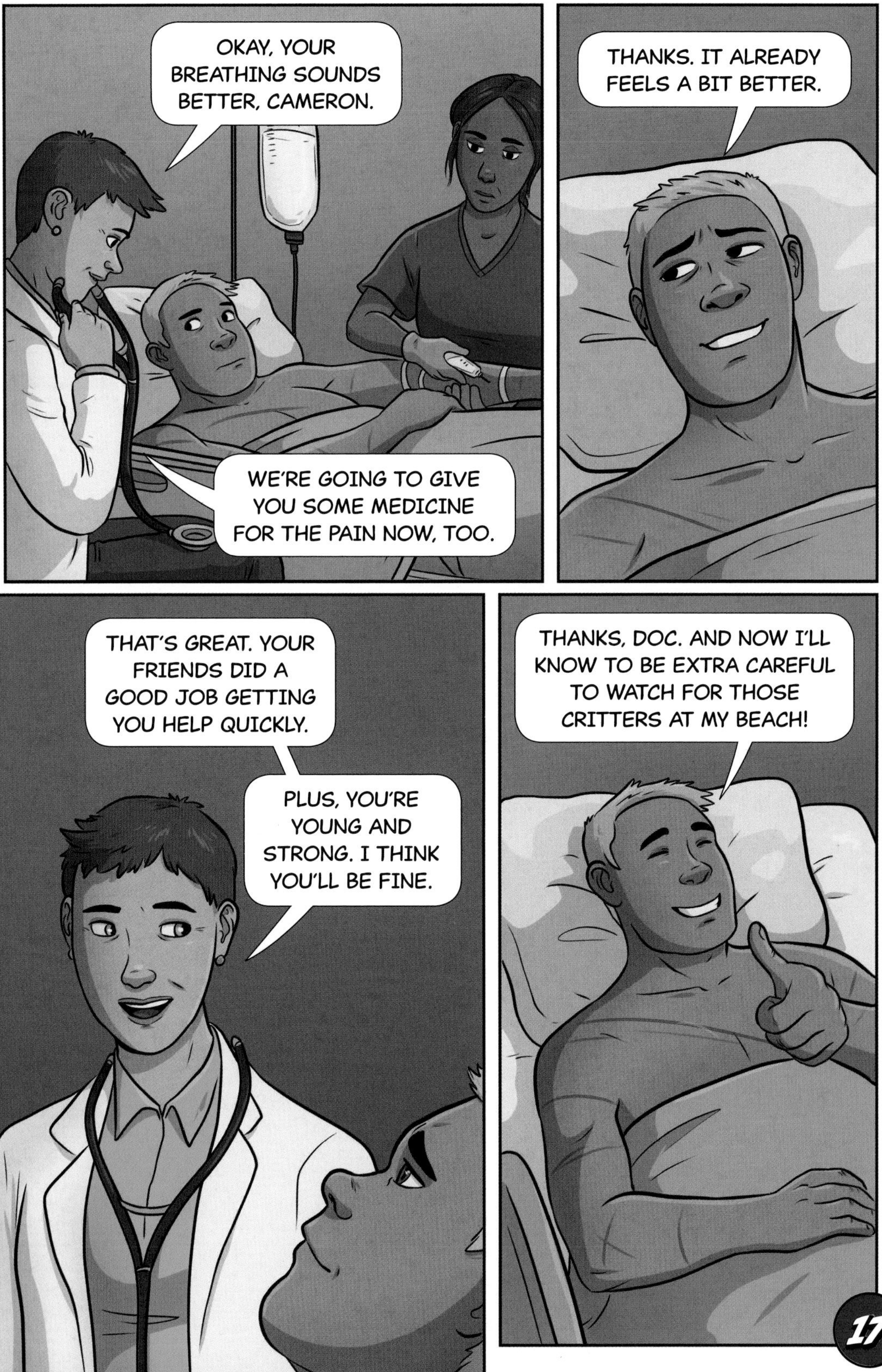
OKAY, YOUR BREATHING SOUNDS BETTER, CAMERON.
WE'RE GOING TO GIVE YOU SOME MEDICINE FOR THE PAIN NOW, TOO.
THANKS. IT ALREADY FEELS A BIT BETTER.
THAT'S GREAT. YOUR FRIENDS DID A GOOD JOB GETTING YOU HELP QUICKLY.
PLUS, YOU'RE YOUNG AND STRONG. I THINK YOU'LL BE FINE.
THANKS, DOC. AND NOW I'LL KNOW TO BE EXTRA CAREFUL TO WATCH FOR THOSE CRITTERS AT MY BEACH!

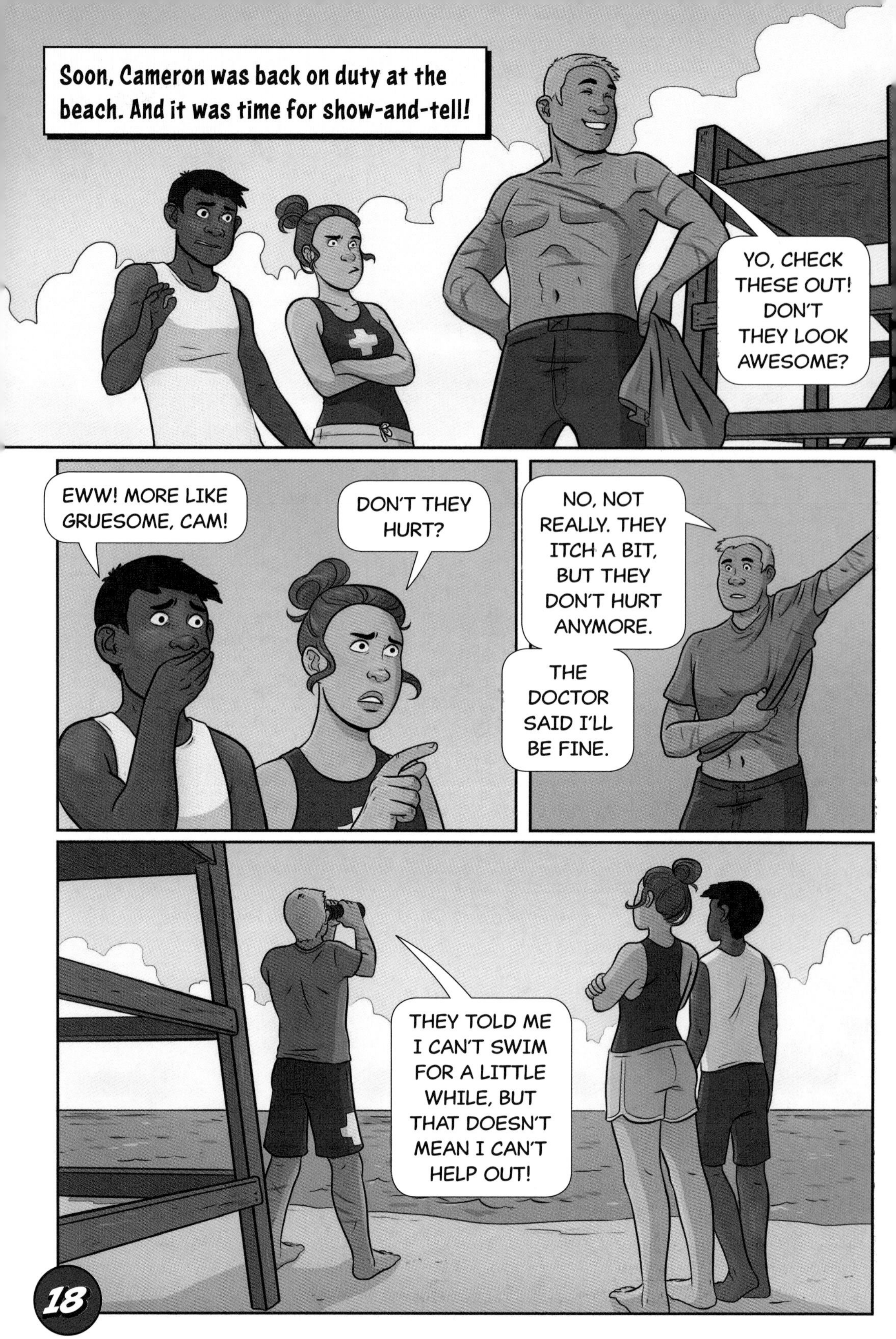
Soon, Cameron was back on duty at the beach. And it was time for show-and-tell!
YO, CHECK THESE OUT! DON'T THEY LOOK AWESOME?
EWW! MORE LIKE GRUESOME, CAM!
DON'T THEY HURT?
NO, NOT REALLY. THEY ITCH A BIT, BUT THEY DON'T HURT ANYMORE.
THE DOCTOR SAID I'LL BE FINE.
THEY TOLD ME I CAN'T SWIM FOR A LITTLE WHILE, BUT THAT DOESN'T MEAN I CAN'T HELP OUT!

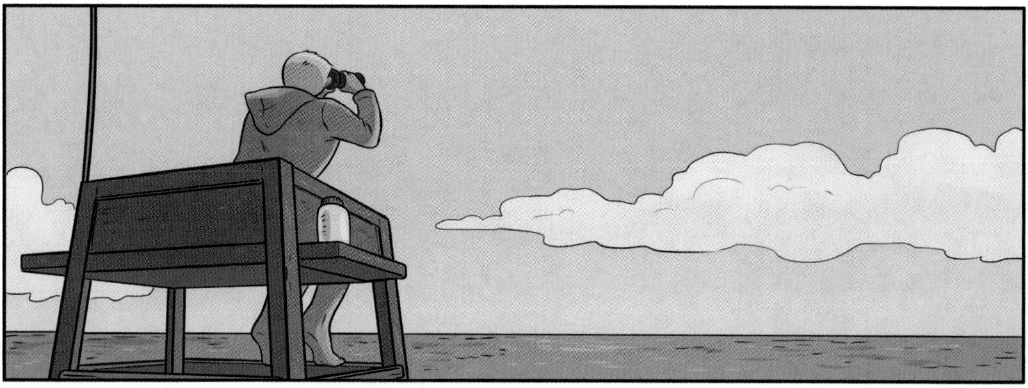

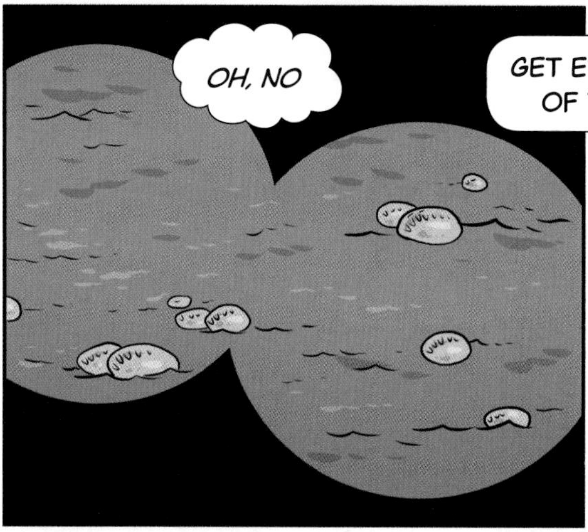
OH, NO

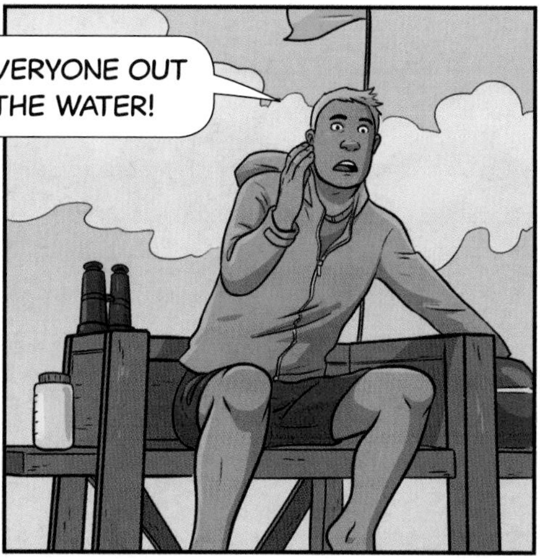
GET EVERYONE OUT OF THE WATER!

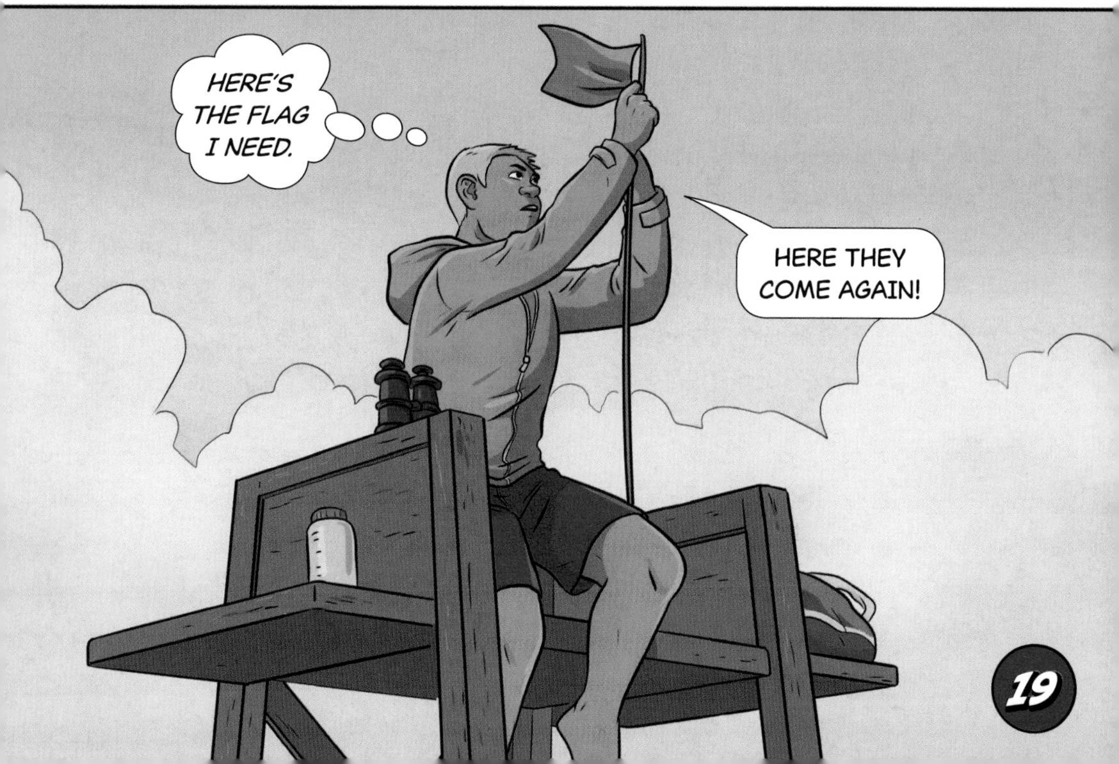
HERE'S THE FLAG I NEED.
HERE THEY COME AGAIN!

ABOUT PORTUGUESE MEN-OF-WAR

A Portuguese man-of-war is not a single animal, but a **colony**—a group of animals that live together and depend on one another to survive. There are four different kinds of **polyps** that make up a man-of-war colony. The float at the top is a large, balloon-like polyp. Many other polyps hang below the float and have different jobs, such as helping to catch and digest food.

PORTUGUESE MEN OF WAR

- The Portuguese man-of-war was named by sailors long ago. Its shape reminded them of the sails on ships from Portugal.

- A man-of-war's tentacles contain thousands of tiny stingers that can shoot **venom** into prey.

- Some tentacles can be as long as 165 feet (50 m).

- These floating colonies live in warm waters all around the world.

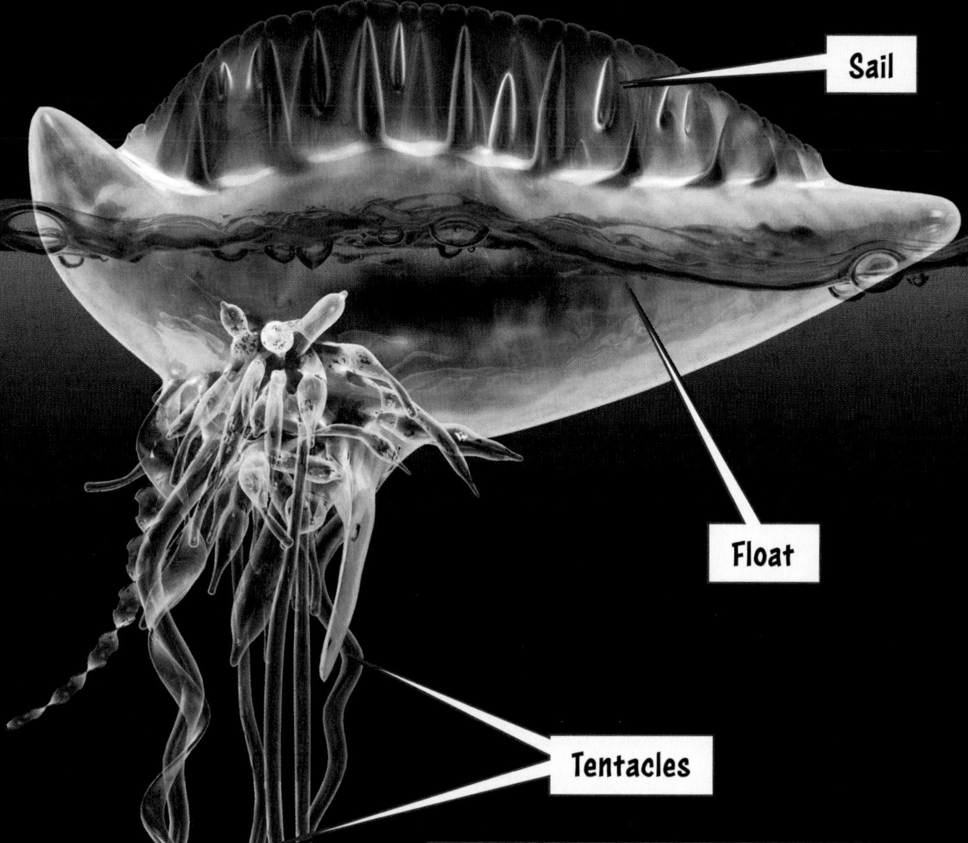
Sail
Float
Tentacles

When the tentacles are touched, tiny stingers inside the tentacles shoot venom into prey.

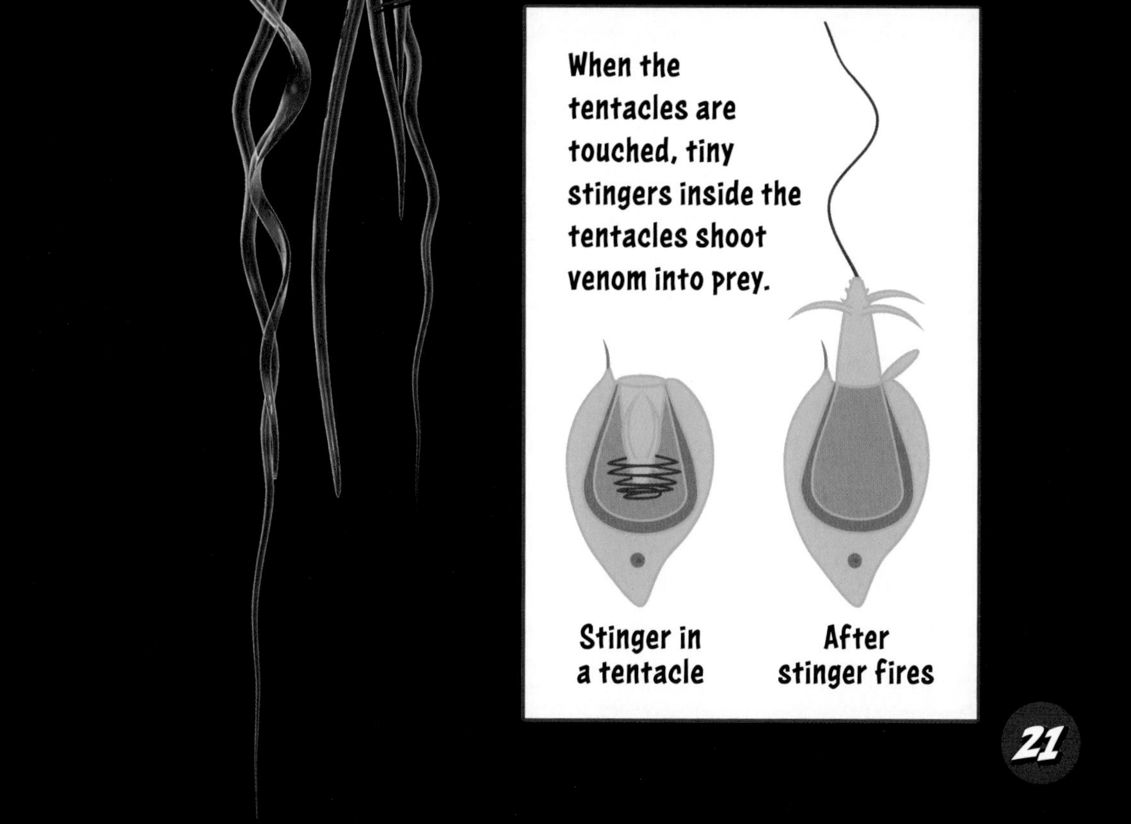

Stinger in a tentacle

After stinger fires

OTHER THINGS
THAT STING

The Portuguese man-of-war can deliver a dangerous sting.
Other kinds of sea creatures also have powerful stings.

SOUTHERN STINGRAYS

- The southern stingray is a fish that has a large, flat body and a long, whiplike tail with one or more sharp stingers.
- The stingers release venom when the animal swings its tail up to attack an enemy.
- People sometimes get stung when they step on a stingray. The pain from a sting can be very bad, and it can take a long time for the wound to heal.

BRISTLEWORMS

- The bristleworm is a kind of sea worm that lives in warm ocean water. It is usually found under rocks and in coral reefs.
- The worms have venom in their hairlike bristles, which can break off and pierce an enemy's skin.
- If a snorkeler or swimmer is stung, the sting causes pain and burning but is not dangerous.

GLOSSARY

colony a group of animals that live together and depend on one another to survive

marine having to do with the ocean

paralyze to cause something to be unable to move

polyps animals that live and work with other polyps to make up one Portuguese man-of-war

prey animals that are hunted by other animals for food

respiration the act or process of breathing

tentacles parts that hang down from a Portuguese man-of-war and can sting other animals

venom poison that some animals can send into the bodies of other animals through a bite or sting

INDEX

READ MORE

Derrick, Stuart and Charlotte Goddard. *World's Strangest Ocean Beasts*. New York: Lonely Planet Kids (2018).

Lunis, Natalie. *Portuguese Man-of-War: Floating Misery (Afraid of the Water)*. New York: Bearport Publishing (2009).

Cazenove, Christophe. *Armed & Dangerous (Sea Creatures in Their Own Words Vol. 2)*. New York: Papercutz (2017).

LEARN MORE ONLINE

1. Go to **www.factsurfer.com**

2. Enter "**Floating Misery**" into the search box.

3. Click on the cover of this book to see a list of websites.